DATE DUE			
FEB 6 1996			
261-9500			PRINTED IN U.S.A.

Romans

Kath Davies

Illustrations by
Harry Clow

A ZOË BOOK

A ZOË BOOK

©1995 Zoë Books Limited

Devised and produced by
Zoë Books Limited
15 Worthy Lane
Winchester
Hampshire SO23 7AB
England

Illustrative material used in this book first appeared in *History Detective: Over 1600 Years Ago In The Roman Empire*, published by Zoë Books Limited.

First published in Great Britain in 1995 by
Zoë Books Limited
15 Worthy Lane
Winchester
Hampshire SO23 7AB

A record of the CIP data is available from the British Library.

ISBN 1 874488 43 6

Printed in Italy by Grafedit SpA
Edited by Denise Allard
Design: Julian Holland & Pardoe Blacker
Production: Grahame Griffiths

Photographic acknowledgements

The publishers wish to acknowledge, with thanks, the following photographic sources:

6 Ronald Sheridan/Ancient Art and Architecture Collection/L Ellison; 7, 10, 11, 15t, 15b, 18, 19, 22, 23 Ronald Sheridan/Ancient Art and Architecture Collection; 27t Ronald Sheridan/Ancient Art and Architecture Collection/Tim Butcher; 27b Ronald Sheridan/Ancient Art and Architecture Collection.

CONTENTS

The Roman Army 4

Roman Roads 8

Towns 12

In the Country 16

Daily Life 20

Entertainment 24

Time Line 28

Glossary 30

Index 32

The Roman Army

About 4000 years ago, a group of people settled in villages near the River Tiber in central Italy. They were called the **Latins**. Their villages were on the paths which **traders** used. The traders bought or exchanged goods with the Latins, who grew rich. The villages spread until they joined to form the city of Rome. The people of Rome chose leaders to rule the city. This way of ruling is called a **republic**.

The republic's strength came from its army. Roman soldiers were sent to **conquer** other peoples. The army fought first in Italy, and then in other lands. By about 2200 years ago, Rome ruled a large **empire** of countries around the Mediterranean Sea.

The army built forts in areas which it had conquered. The forts were like small towns. They were all built to the same plan.

Inside a strong fence or wall there were buildings where the soldiers ate and slept. The officers had separate houses. There were stables for horses, and stores for food. There was a hospital, and offices for the people who ruled the area.

Roman soldiers

The Roman army was made up of foot soldiers called **legions**. There were about 5000 men in a legion. Each legion contained ten smaller groups, called **cohorts**. The cohort was divided into groups of 100 men, or centuries.

The army took in troops called auxilia from the countries which it conquered. Some of these troops fought on horseback.

Each legion carried a silver eagle. It stood for the power of the legion.

▼ The Roman fort at Housesteads, in northern England. Soldiers at this fort protected **Hadrian's Wall**. The Romans built this wall across the country.

The Romans left behind many clues which tell us how they lived. Some of their roads and buildings can still be seen. Pots, coins and tools have been found in places where they ruled.

Find out if the Romans left anything behind in the area where you live.

HISTORY STARTERS

Many Romans wrote about their lives. They also wrote about Rome's history, and how Rome ruled its people. The writer Plutarch tells us about the Roman army.

▲ Augustus was the first emperor of Rome. He chose a group of the finest soldiers to be the **Praetorian Guard**. Their duty was to guard the emperor.

▶ The Emperor Trajan built this column to show a great victory. Here soldiers are building a fort.

Roman Roads

When the Romans conquered a country, such as Britain, they built roads. The roads were straight, so that the soldiers could march quickly.

The Roman road planners marked out the shortest, flattest routes with poles. Then soldiers dug a trench about one metre deep. They put large stones at the bottom of the trench, then smaller stones on top. The stones made a strong base for the road.

The surfaces of the roads were made in different ways. In busy places, such as towns, the surfaces were made of large, flat paving stones. Other roads had small pebbles on top. The pebbles were pressed down by heavy carts, and by the marching soldiers.

There were long kerbstones at the sides of the roads. They kept the road stones in place. Ditches were built beside the roads.

Roman roads were built with a curved surface. Rain water ran off the surface into the ditches.

Travel across the empire

Many Roman roads can still be seen. We know how they were built because people have studied them. People who study the things which other people have left behind are called **archaeologists**.

Roman roads stretched for more than 53 000 miles across the empire. They were built so well that some modern roads have been laid down on top of them.

Traders and **merchants** used the roads. They carried their goods in carts or on donkeys. Merchants sent goods by road and by ship to Rome. They sent corn from north Africa. Pottery, cloth, metals and **slaves** came from other parts of the Roman Empire.

▲ Roman road planners used an instrument called a groma. They used it to make sure that the road poles were in straight lines.

◀ This Roman road is called the Appian Way. It ran for 130 miles between Rome and Capua. Some of it can still be seen.

Roman ships

Paintings, carvings and wrecks show us that **cargo ships** were of different sizes.

Some cargo ships were large. They could be about 30 metres long and 9 metres wide. They carried grain, oil or stone over long distances. These ships sailed at speeds of more than 4 miles an hour.

We do not know much about Roman warships, because no wrecks or remains have been found. However, there are wall carvings which show some warships called triremes. These ships had three sets of oars.

Roman sailors found their way by watching the Sun and the stars.

The wrecks of many Roman cargo ships have been found in the mud of sea or river beds. In some wrecks, coins have been found.

What could the coins tell us about the ship?

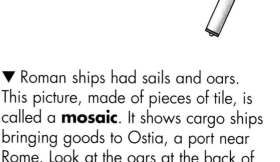

▼ Roman ships had sails and oars. This picture, made of pieces of tile, is called a **mosaic**. It shows cargo ships bringing goods to Ostia, a port near Rome. Look at the oars at the back of the ships. They are the steering oars.

Towns

The first Roman towns grew out of villages. They were not planned. About 2000 years ago, around the year 50 BC, the Romans began to follow the Greek style of town planning.

Many Roman towns had two main streets. The streets met in the middle to form crossroads. There was an open market, called a **forum**, where the two roads met.

Roman towns had fine public buildings, such as the **basilica**, which was used as the town hall and law courts. There were also inns, temples and bath-houses, as well as shops, houses and a theatre.

Games were held in a building called an **amphitheatre**.

Water was brought to towns from rivers or lakes. It flowed along channels, or **aqueducts**. The town's waste was carried away in tunnels, or **sewers**.

City streets

The streets of Rome were narrow and winding. They smelled of bad drains. More than a million people lived and worked in the city.

▼ In Ancient Rome, the houses were very close together. There were often fires, which spread very quickly.

The people emptied rubbish into the streets. There were many diseases. The streets were so crowded that carts were not allowed into the city by day. It was very noisy, even at night.

People were not allowed to be buried inside Roman towns. They were buried along the roads outside the towns.

The basilica stood on one side of the open market place. On the other three sides there was a covered walkway, with shops and offices. In the centre, there might be fountains and statues. Traders sold their goods here, while jugglers and acrobats entertained the crowds.

The Roman town, Pompeii, was buried suddenly, by a **volcano**. Archaeologists have uncovered the streets and houses.

What can we learn about the Romans from the things which were found at Pompeii?

HISTORY STARTERS

▲ Town streets were often muddy. These stepping stones are at **Pompeii**.

▶ A Roman butcher is chopping meat. Joints of meat hang from hooks in the shop.

IN THE COUNTRY

In the Country

This picture shows a Roman country
house, called a villa. Many rich families owned
country houses and farms. They did not live there
all the time. They lived in the cities, and visited their
villas when they wanted a holiday away from the town.
A manager ran the farm with many workers or slaves.

The farms provided food for their owners and workers.
They grew vegetables, and crops such as wheat. There
were olive trees for olive oil, and grapes for wine. Cattle,
sheep, pigs and chickens were kept.

The farm buildings were often next to the family's villa. There were stables for the horses, and stores for the farm tools. The slaves and other farm workers lived near the stables.

The wheat crop was stored in a barn called a granary. Wine was kept in a cool room.

Many farmers grew more food than they needed. They sold the extra food, and became rich.

▼ This mosaic shows hunters with a wild boar.

Hadrian's villa

The emperor Hadrian owned a villa at Tivoli, near Rome. It had a library, baths and a theatre, as well as many rooms. The house was heated by a fire which warmed the air underneath the floors.

In fine houses like Hadrian's, there were pictures on the walls and floors. Some pictures were mosaics. They were made of thousands of small pieces of coloured stone.

◀ The gardens at Hadrian's villa. There were fountains and a pool, with statues of people and animals.

Work on the farm

The Romans have left us many clues about life in the country. Writers such as Cato tell us about work on a farm. The poet Virgil wrote poems about country life. Artists painted pictures on walls. In Rome there is a stone carving which shows the work on a farm through the year.

In March and November, people sowed wheat. In June they cut the hay, and in October they picked the grapes. December was the time for picking olives, and for collecting firewood.

Roman farmers grew beans, carrots, cabbages and lettuce. The remains of some of these vegetables have been found in ancient rubbish heaps!

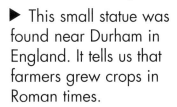

The Roman writer, Pliny, lived in a villa near the sea. Pliny wrote letters to his friends about his daily life. Pretend you are Pliny. Write a letter to a friend about your villa.

HISTORY STARTERS

▶ This small statue was found near Durham in England. It tells us that farmers grew crops in Roman times.

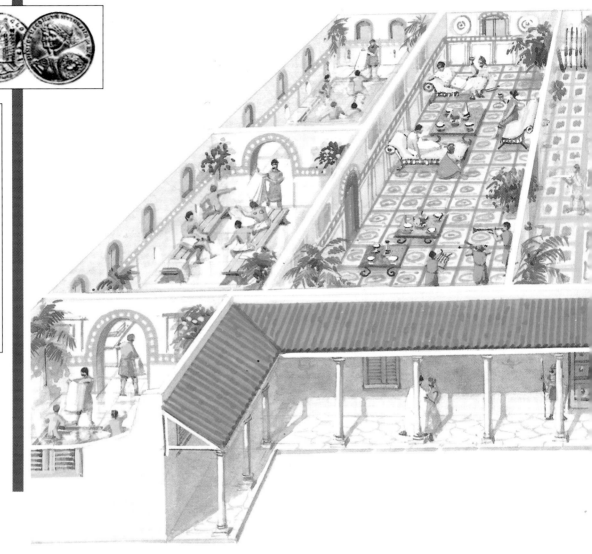

Daily Life

This picture shows a town house, called a **domum**. A rich family owned many slaves and servants. They did the daily work of the house, such as the cooking and the cleaning.

Most town houses had rooms around a small, open courtyard. The courtyard was covered with **canvas** in wet or cold weather. From the outside, the house looked plain. However, the rooms were often full of wall pictures, mosaics and statues. Many houses had gardens with trees and **herbs**.

Women in rich families did not work outside the home. Most wealthy women ran their large houses and brought up their children at home. Many women were married by the time they were 14 or 15 years old. Their husbands and sons might be soldiers, or work in offices.

In other families, women worked in shops or markets. They spun wool and wove cloth at home. Their husbands were usually craftworkers. They might be potters or tool-makers, jewellers or woodworkers.

People who were educated, but not rich, might work as doctors or teachers.

▲ This carving shows some pupils reading to their teacher.

At the age of six, some Roman children started school. They used a wax tablet and a metal pen called a stylus to learn to read and write. They also learned history, geography, geometry and public speaking.

Make a list of some different ways in which we write things down today.

HISTORY STARTERS

Food

Wall pictures and carvings show how the cooks worked. Their knives, tools, pots and pans were very like those which we use today. Many Roman kitchen **utensils** have been found.

▼ This picture is drawn from a Roman carving. It shows people at dinner and slaves working in the kitchen.

Rich Romans ate and drank a great deal of food and wine. Dinner might start with salad, eggs and vegetables, then fish or meat with sauces. Fruit, nuts, ices and sweets followed.

There were dishes made of glass, silver or gold. People ate with their fingers. Slaves brought bowls of scented water to wash the guests' hands.

◀ The hot springs at Bath in England are famous. The Romans built a bath-house here.

▼ At a bath-house, people had their bodies massaged with scented oil. They also had their nails cut and polished. This is called a manicure.

Many Roman towns had bath-houses which all the people could use. There were cold pools and hot pools. The water for the hot pools was warmed by fires. Some very rich people had baths in their own homes.

Entertainment

About 1500 years ago, Roman people enjoyed more than 200 days of holiday each year! Their slaves did all the hard work. Many Romans spent their time meeting friends in the public gardens or the forum. They went to the baths and to the theatre. They watched **chariot** races, or fights between animals and men called gladiators.

The city of Rome held the largest race track in the empire. It was called the Circus Maximus, which means 'Great Circle'. This track held about 250 000 people, and was 550 metres long.

People went to see Rome's four famous racing clubs. Each club had its own colours. There were up to 24 races each day. After every race, there were clowns, jugglers, acrobats and fire-eaters to watch.

Racing was dangerous. Many drivers and horses died. Drivers who won became rich and famous.

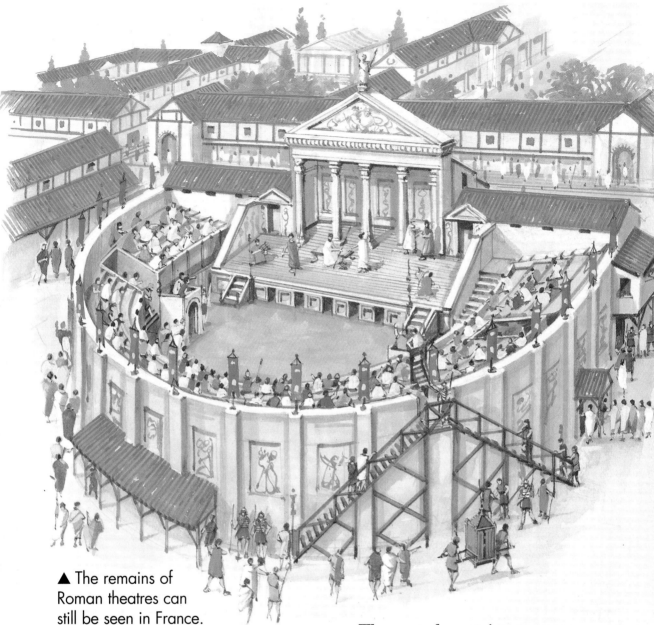

▲ The remains of Roman theatres can still be seen in France.

At the theatre

The first plays were performed in Rome about 2300 years ago. They were held in small wooden theatres. As plays became more popular, larger, stone theatres were built. Some of the biggest theatres held about 27 000 people. We can still see some of these theatres today.

The people sat in rows, one above the other. The best seats were at the front. Rich and important people, such as the Roman leaders, sat there. The poorest people sat at the top, far away from the stage.

The actors and actresses wore masks. Some performers were slaves. They earned a lot of money if they became popular.

▶ Gladiators fought each other. They also fought wild animals, such as leopards and lions. Mosaics show us these fights.

Fighting games took place at amphitheatres. Bears, bulls and other animals fought there.

Two gladiators would fight until one of them was killed. They also fought animals. Gladiators were often slaves, who were specially trained. If they won a fight, they might also win their freedom.

Sometimes, people who had been sentenced to death were put into the arena to be killed by the wild animals.

Some Roman writers hated these cruel sports. Seneca said that the crowds shouted for more and more people to die. Juvenal said that the people wanted free 'bread and circuses'. They did not care about anything else.

▼ The Coliseum in Rome was a famous amphitheatre. It held 50 000 people.

Time Line

BC

2000	The Latin people settled in central Italy.
800	The Latins built villages on seven hills near the River Tiber. The villages grew and became the city of Rome.
509	Rome became a Republic.
58	Julius Caesar began the Roman conquest of Gaul (France).
55–54	Julius Caesar crossed to Britain from Gaul.
27	The first emperor, Augustus, came to power.

AD

43	The Roman invasion of Britain.
61	Queen Boudicca led the fight against the Romans in southeast Britain.
64	The Great Fire of Rome. The Emperor Nero blamed the Christians for the fire. Many Christians were put to death.
79	Pompeii was buried under ash from the volcano, Vesuvius.
122	Hadrian's Wall was built across Britain.

238–284 Wars break out throughout the Roman Empire.

312 The Emperor Constantine became a Christian.406 The Roman legions left Britain.

410 The city of Rome was attacked by people from the northeast – the Visigoths.

455 The Vandals attacked and destroyed Rome.

476 The last Roman emperor, Romulus Augustulus, was overthrown.

Glossary

amphitheatre: a place where fighting games were held. They were usually built outside the town walls.

aqueduct: a channel, or canal, that carries water. Sometimes the Romans built bridges to carry the aqueducts. Some Roman aqueducts can still be seen today.

archaeologist: someone who studies the remains of buildings and objects, to find out how people lived.

basilica: the large building like a town hall. It held offices and law courts. Traders often met here.

BC: Before the birth of Christ. In the Christian calendar, years are counted before or after Christ was born. AD stands for Anno Domini which means 'in the year of our Lord'. AD shows that the year was after the birth of Christ.

canvas: strong cloth made from the stems of plants called flax and hemp. The Romans used it to make sails.

cargo ships: ships which carry goods.

chariot: a small cart or carriage pulled by horses.

cohort: a group, or unit, of soldiers in the Roman Army. There were about 600 men in a cohort.

conquer: to take power after winning a war, and rule the people and the country that lost the war.

domum: a Roman town house.

empire: many different countries or lands that are ruled from another country. The man who rules the empire is called the **emperor**.

fort: an army camp with a wall around it.

forum: the square at the centre of a Roman town.

Hadrian's Wall: a stone wall which Hadrian had built across northern England to protect Roman Britain from attacks by the Scots. Hadrian was one of the most famous Roman emperors. He lived from AD76 to AD138.

herbs: plants which were used to add flavour to food, or to make medicines.

Latin: the name of the people who settled in central Italy. Also the name of the language spoken by the Romans.

legion: a section of the Roman army – about 5000 men.

merchants: people who earn a living by buying and selling things from many different countries. Merchants often travel far away from home to do this.

mosaic: a design, or picture, made out of thousands of tiny bits of coloured stone or glass. Many Roman buildings had floors made of mosaic.

Pompeii: a town near Naples in central Italy. It was buried by hot ash from the **volcano** Vesuvius in AD79. Most of the people who lived there died when they were covered in the ash.

Praetorian Guard: the finest soldiers in the Roman army. It was their job to guard the emperor.

republic: a country which has no king or queen. The people vote for their rulers. Rome became a republic in about 510BC. In 27BC, Octavian became the first Roman emperor. He was called Augustus.

sewers: large pipes which carry away dirty water and other waste.

slaves: people who were bought and sold by other people. Slaves had to work for their owners. They were not paid for the work they did. Slaves were not free to choose who they worked for or where they lived.

traders: people who earn a living by buying and selling things. Traders sometimes travelled around the countryside to do this.

utensils: tools and containers used in the kitchen.

volcano: a mountain which throws out melted rock and hot ash.

Index

amphitheatre 13, 27
archaeologists 10, 15
army 4–10, 26

baths 13, 18, 23, 24
burial 14

children 21, 22
craftworkers 21
crops 16, 17, 19

disease 14

emperors 6, 7, 18, 28, 29

farms 16, 17, 19
food 5, 15, 16, 17, 19, 22
forts 5, 6

games 13, 24, 27
gladiators 24, 27

heating 18, 23
holidays 16, 24
houses 5, 13, 14, 15, 16, 17,
    18, 20–21, 22–23

Latins 4, 28
legions 6

markets 12, 15, 21
merchants 10
mosaics 11, 18, 20, 27

Pompeii 15

races 24, 25
roads 8, 9, 10, 12, 14
Roman Empire 5, 10, 28
Rome 4, 5, 7, 10, 14, 18, 25,
26, 27, 28, 29

school 22
sewers 13
ships 10, 11
shops 13, 15, 21
slaves 10, 16, 17, 20, 22, 24,
    26, 27

theatre 13, 18, 24, 26
tools 7, 17, 22
towns 5, 9, 12–15, 16
trade 4, 10, 11, 14, 15
transport 8–11

warships 11
women 21
writers 7, 19, 27